DIV♥RCE:

The Unspoken Childhood Trauma

TARA SEALS

ISBN: 9780578880136

Printed in the United States of America

Published by Able Publishing

Editor: L.B. Cadogan

Dedication

I want to dedicate this book to my mama, granny, and my fourth grade teacher, Mrs. Forestine Owens.

Mama, thank you for your unyielding love, guidance, and perseverance. You showed me through your strength how to never give up. Your tough love is understood and much appreciated. You are my reason why. Love you always and forever.

Granny, honey, I can't believe I am in my right mind without you living here with me on this earth, but you show up every day in subtle ways. Thank you for always teaching me the importance of being exactly who I am—unapologetically. I appreciate you for being such a gentle soul that I could always depend on, no matter what. Our secrets, girl talks, strolls in the malls and boutiques, church outfits...I could go on and on. Missing you like crazy. Love you, Ida Mae.

Oh, Mrs. Owens! Thank you for letting me jump into your arms once I arrived to school, and sometimes just lay on your shoulder and cry. I didn't know exactly what was happening at home, and I needed an outlet the same way adults do. You listened attentively and shared the best advice ever! I am now an educator and understand the importance of being there for my students. I appreciate and love you for going above and beyond when I needed you most.

Table of Contents

Introduction

"Mama! Come look! My bathroom is all black and I love it! Even the sink, tub, and toilet are black! Mama, I can't wait to move into our new house!" Moving day came and my mama got everything moved in and we settled into our new home. My brother and I each had our own room, so my mama purchased new bedding and furniture for us. I was so excited! A new house always meant new friends and I rarely had a problem making friends with my personality.

Our house sat on a cul-de-sac and there were lots of kids; playing outside was always an adventure! I met a girl named Sarah and she had a bike. We would have bike races, play with our Barbie dolls, and make figurines with dirt and water. Sarah was a round-faced girl with glasses that she hated. Years later, I had to wear glasses and wondered why she hated them so much! They became a part of my daily fashion statement. YASSSSSS!

One day we pulled up to our house and my mama took the groceries out of the car. I assisted her and grabbed my little brother's hand. When we got to the door, there was a note on it. Mama read a little bit, grabbed it, and we proceeded to go inside the house and put away the groceries. My mama called my daddy and was like, "What is this about? Why haven't you paid the rent?" It was an eviction notice from the sheriff's department saying we had thirty days to move. *Oh no!* I thought to myself. I was furious! Why did I have to leave a neighborhood I loved and my black bathroom—I certainly wasn't ready to give that up! All of this happened while my daddy, still married to my mama, was living with another woman. I just couldn't make sense of it all. This was a lot for a young child like myself to process, but I did and realized that my life as I knew it was about to change forever.

This book is a true story about my life and how my parents' divorce and the events surrounding it caused childhood trauma. Childhood trauma is the experience of an event by a child that is emotionally painful or distressful. I had to learn that talking about my experience isn't speaking ill of my father, but not talking about my experience doesn't protect him either. Sharing my experience, however, helps us all to understand that children are standing by, paying attention, and watching everything unfold. These children will one day become adults and time can never be duplicated.

Chapter 1

The Unexpected

Moving day came and we moved into an apartment—on the third floor, might I add. I also had to share a room with my baby brother. I was so upset and wanted answers to so many questions, but I was a child and I had to stay in a child's place with adult bullshit swarming around in my head.

The apartment was nice and cozy, and something my mama could afford on her own without depending on my daddy to pay the rent, so I accepted the fact that my mama was doing what she had to do. As a matter of fact, I realized in that very moment that my mama was a strong, Black woman, and no matter what happened, she kept it moving. She was selfless and resilient; always putting us first, and she *never* folded.

It was my daddy's weekend, and he came to pick us up in his brand-spanking-new, red Mazda single cab two-seater truck with his "Kappa Alpha Psi" tag on the front. *She* purchased it for him. The first thing I said to myself was, *where will me and my brother sit?* He came around and put us in the truck and my brother sat in my lap. I pulled the seatbelt across us and we were on our way. I had a lot to say...boy, my 8-year-old mind was going! Pissed was an understatement.

Why would you agree to accepting this "gift" if there wasn't enough room for us to ride with you safely? You are that obsessed with things that you couldn't speak up for us and say, 'thank you, but no thank you?' This is a nice truck, but I am not able to safely transport my two kids. Of course not, he was ALL about him and that showed through his actions.

In that moment, I was furious with my daddy because he didn't speak up for us... yet again. This is our safety we are talking about and it was sacrificed all because he couldn't say no. Growing up around my grandpa made me appreciate how he spoke up for his family. I loved the fact that my grandpa didn't play about what was his at all. This action also proved something else that had been on my mind...he would never speak up for us because that would mess up his pimpin'!

Unfortunately, I had a daddy that could be bought. This woman was willing to buy him for whatever his price tag was and she did just that! This was a valuable lesson that served its purpose later on in my life when it came to dealing with men—I couldn't be bought, no matter the price. My daddy was selling his soul to the devil and he didn't even know it, but here I am, an 8-year-old little girl, and I had it figured out to a "T".

The move to this new apartment was quite different because I no longer had the luxury of going outside and playing with friends in the cul-de-sac where my mama could easily see us out of our big, picture-sized window. I was now limited to a third-floor view with a Big Star grocery store across the street, and my mama rarely let us play outside in our huge apartment complex. She wasn't comfortable with the idea, so we resorted to playing in the living room, which offered more open space since we were cramped in a room together and had very little space between our twin-size beds.

As we concluded our normal routine of school and work one Friday evening, my mama grabbed us some takeout and we headed home. We watched TV and took my mama up on her rare invitation to sleep in her bed. Boy, were we excited! Snuggled in tight, we slept the night away until mama abruptly woke us up saying, "Put your shoes on, we gotta get out of here!"

Little did we know, our entire apartment was on fire! It was a 3-alarm fire, and we were one of the few families left within our 24-unit apartment building that was not out safely due to our faulty smoke detector. My mama looked down at us and said, "Look, I am going to have to throw you both out of the window one at a time, and then I am going to jump." Confused and not sure what question to ask first, I simply didn't ask any at all. But I knew my mama meant serious business. She said, "Someone down below on the ground will catch you. And I want both of you to know that I love you very much."

Mama proceeded to open the window, reached for my brother, and threw him out the window. Someone caught him before reaching the ground. Then she threw me out of the window and someone caught me. But of course, as a child knowing that your mama chose to throw her children to safety first, we were concerned about whether or not she would make it to safety. As soon as my feet touched the ground after being caught by the rescuers, I turned to the window my brother and I were just thrown from to make sure my mama was still holding on and ready to jump to rejoin our little family.

I saw her climb on top of the window sill, which made me sad and relieved all at the same time and jump out of the window to safety. The rescuers weren't able to catch her as she jumped from the fiery building because she dropped to the ground in more of a sideways motion, but they did manage to break her fall. She made it out, which was most important, but suffered from injuries as a result.

That night was life changing as you could imagine.While we were jumping and being thrown out of the window of a burning apartment building, my dad was laying in his cozy bed with her and their new baby less than a mile away.

My parents were still married and I didn't understand why we had to be subjected to the foolery of adult folly. The unexpected was happening in every area of my life. I encountered difficulties at school, had to stay with *her* and my daddy for a week while my mama recovered from the injuries she sustained in the fire, was presented with a "new" little brother that I didn't understand how he was my brother and didn't come from my mama, and was reminded daily for an entire week that my little brother and I were staying in the "guest" bedroom. I felt lost, and most of all angry that my family as I once knew it was falling apart.

Takeaways

1) Check on your older children. They usually mask their trauma better because they are the example for the other sibling(s), and they know this because they have been told time and time again. Whew, the struggle is real.

2) Although you may be going through hell and back as a parent during the time of drama in your life, it is necessary for you to find the proper assistance you need to be the best version of yourself at a time your child needs you most. Remember, once you have children, your life is no longer yours. It becomes a shared entity and your number one priority becomes your child, which comes with millions of sacrifices due to the decision alone.

Chapter 2

No Explanation

New woman, new baby? Where did these people come from and why are they here? I had questions and I needed answers. So, who better to get the answer from than the horse itself? As a little girl growing up in the South and being raised Southern Baptist, I was always taught to stay in a child's place. Although my mama knew how I felt about this whole "arrangement," she told me to always be respectful when I went over my daddy's house.

Well, on this particular day, all of that went out of the window and my little 8-year-old-self faced my daddy's *sidechick* while he was still married to my mama. She was sitting on the end of the couch rocking the new baby and I sat on the opposite end of the couch. I said, "I have a question for you."

"Okay, what's your question?" she said.

"But first, I want to turn my back to you," I said. In my mind, this would be the "most polite" way to ask her this audacious question.

"Okay," she said.

I turned around and asked her, "So how would you feel if someone had a baby by your husband?"

The room fell silent—you could hear a rat piss on cotton as my granny used to say. She wasn't ready for this question at all, but I patiently waited as I was now facing her, with my legs and arms crossed, waiting for an answer. Of course being *her*, she never answered the question, but instead danced around it acting as if I was the crazy one. Later that week, I asked my daddy for the third or fourth time, why. He didn't have an answer either.

This lesson came early in life. Sometimes there isn't an explanation. You learn that some people do not have the wherewithal to admit to their wrongdoing and you sometimes have to forgive a person who wasn't even sorry.

So here I am, asking questions, getting no answers, yet being subjected to be around *her*

EVERY time I went to visit my daddy. I didn't understand her role, why they lived together, why she had to participate in EVERY activity we did, why her opinion mattered about where we ate dinner, and furthermore why she mattered at all. Who was this person and why did my daddy leave us for *her*? As life unfolded, I received all the answers and then some.

Takeaways

1) Engage in thorough conversations with your children. Of course, we know you are the adult, but understand that your decisions are affecting their lives. Be honest and explain to them what is

going on and why things have changed. This will not only help them understand what is playing out in front of them, but it takes the guesswork out of the situation and helps them understand the complexities of relationships.

2) Visits to the non-custodial parent's home can be a quite uncomfortable position to be in as a child. If the non-custodial parent has a significant other, they should spend a portion of time strictly with the child; if not, all of it. Time is limited and precious might I add, so spend as much time as you can with your child alone. Get to know

them, teach them a skill, create amazing experiences and leave your "other" out of the mix. They are truly coming to see YOU. Make the best out of each visit as they are numbered. Remember, once children begin to get older and more active in extracurricular activities and other interests, time will be even more limited. Do not let time pass you by.

Chapter 3

In & Out

Children have feelings too, but more often than not, they are not asked of their opinion, nor do they usually offer it without question, so what ends up happening? Emotional trauma that is never-ending unless an observant adult steps in to assist the child in the areas of concern. Most of the time, children begin to show what's going on on the inside on the outside. This can be portrayed in several ways such as depression, conduct disorders, delinquency, negative impact on overall personal or academic development, and the list goes on. Some children feel as if the dismantling of their family is their fault.

At some point during my parents' separation that led to divorce, I felt all of these feelings. I just couldn't believe that my brother and I were not worth fighting for and simultaneously we were forced to accept another woman and a new sibling. Children should not be subjected to accept your *new* anything, especially when the lines have not been made clear as to what the new situation is going to be with the parents.

It was an in-and-out situation for my mama and daddy. When he was "in," it gave me hope that my family would soon be back to normal, but when he was "out," my world crumbled into pieces all over again, so the wound that was created due to his infidelities were opened and closed repeatedly. It penetrated my heart worse and worse each time he failed to give me what I loved more than anything...my family.

I was that little girl that absolutely adored her father, even accompanying him to the barber shop for his weekly barber visits to see Ms. Evelyn. Our connection was so deep that I sat in his lap as he relished in his grooming routine. Music was also something that connected us because my daddy played his music loud, just like I liked it! At any given moment during our ride through the city streets—The O'Jay's, Curtis Mayfield, The Temptations, Lenny Williams, and the list goes on—would blare through the speakers as we chewed on his favorite gum, Big Red. Oh and grocery store visits with him were like an unlimited invitation to foodie paradise! Our trips to the mall were inundated with bags of the latest fashion because he believed in looking good. Daddy always smelled good too and everywhere we went, the ladies would smile at him and he would reciprocate...he was definitely a lady's man.

As I played the hand that I was dealt, I visited the confines of his mind with my questions as to why he couldn't stay. I would hold on to his leg and cry with everything in me for him to stay, but my screams of love went unnoticed. His little red truck would disappear into the night, leaving us once again in our apartment to arrive at the home of his "new" family.

The in-and-out game he played lasted for a while until my mama realized that he was doing exactly what he wanted to do, and she had to make an executive decision for her children. The weekly/bi-weekly "slumber parties" ended, and weekend visits—if they happened—became our new norm.

Takeaways

1) If adults want to indulge in dysfunction, that's fine. Children, however, are watching and paying attention to you way more than you give them credit for. Therefore, understand that your actions speak way louder than your words.

2) If you are back and forth between relationships, or you know it's just an entanglement, leave the children out of it. Your adult emotions may be able to deal with the revolving door. A child however, not so much. It only creates a confusing dynamic filled with lost hope and empty promises.

Chapter 4

What is Child Support Exactly?

Child Support is an ongoing, periodic payment (usually monthly) made by a parent for the financial benefit of a child. It is a payment paid directly or indirectly by an *obligor* to an *obligee* for the care and support of a child from a relationship that has been terminated, or in some cases never existed. Often the obligor is the non-custodial parent. The obligee is typically a custodial parent, a caregiver, a guardian, or the state per Google. And this is EXACTLY what it is.

However, I came face-to-face with these words "child support" more times than I could EVER count because my daddy ranted and complained non-stop about it; spewing each word C-H-I-L-D S-U-P-P-O-R-T as if they were the most despicable words ever known to mankind! As a child, I didn't know what that meant, but later understood why he was so angry.

As a well-groomed man, my daddy made sure he "stayed on his toes" because the attention he got from women stroked his ego—he LOVED it. In order to get shiny things, you have to spend money. So, money going out of his check to give to my mama to help with us and that he couldn't control? He clearly wasn't too happy with the divorce settlement amount he was ordered to pay

in child support and he let me know quite often...
even as an adult. But what he failed to understand
was the following: 1) we were never evicted or
lived without lights, gas, or water—we always
had a nice and clean place to stay; 2) we never
went hungry; 3) I was a super involved child and
extracurricular activities cost EXTRA money; 4)
we always had a car—even that hideous dookie-
brown Maverick that back-fired; 5) my mama was
present, never just dropping us off anywhere with
just some ol' anybody; 6) she never complained—
not one time; 7) and more than anything, he was
having this conversation with the *wrong* person.

Now, are there some individuals in the
world that choose to misuse these funds for
frivolous purchases that have nothing to do with

the child? Absolutely. BUT, that's why we have to be careful who we breed with. Most of the time we know who is in front of us, we just don't want to admit it. Good sex can do that to you...gotsta to be mo' careful! Or hell, maybe it wasn't good, and you lost all the way around. It's cool, we all take an "L" every once in a while.

As a man or woman, I suggest you find out the laws where you or your significant other resides if you are considering having a child. This will save you a lot of time and money on the other side because shit can get real ugly real fast in the world of child support. Have a discussion with your partner before having a child so everyone is clear on the expectations, if there are any. Communication rules the nation and if a child is born, he/she has to be taken care of. Some way, somehow.

Takeaways

1) Children are expensive and they have needs that must be met. If you are not ready to support a child financially, you may want to find you another hobby or have sex as safely as possible. However, the only one hundred percent way to make sure you don't have any is to be one hundred percent abstinent. Let's be real, that's probably not going to happen, so review those laws. If it is worth it, do your thing. No judgment here.

2) Don't expect $30,000 a month from a man when he only makes $30,000 a year. Some men are paid child support too. Same rule applies. Each state has their own set of rules. Reading is fundamental.

3) Talking to the child about your adult issues is not going to solve your problem. Plus, it's pretty whack. They would much rather spend quality time with you instead of being a punching bag for your words because you aren't able to properly handle your affairs with the mother of your child. Two words: Man up.

Chapter 5

Presence Not Presents

Prior to receiving his brand-spanking-new truck, my daddy would park his blue Monte Carlo and walk me into the school building hand-in-hand. You couldn't tell me nothing when I was with my daddy. I always remembered to get my thirty cents for my grape juice and a tight hug. Once things got rocky, this memory faded to black and instead of daily, it became every once in a while. I missed his presence and for a little girl, positive masculine energy is necessary.

When it is not available, girls sometimes yearn for that attention from other men that may not have their best interest at heart. As an educator, I have seen this need of attention from a male more times than I care to admit.

I felt lonely, rejected, and furthermore, abandoned. I had a set of expectations for my daddy and he disappointed me. I couldn't believe he picked someone over his own children all because the relationship with him and my mother had dissolved. It was hard putting these pieces of my life as I knew it back together because the adults had made their decision, but it left me disconcerted.

My granny was the glue for me. She was patient, calm, and explained to me what was happening although I preferred to hear from the two people in my life that were creating this uprooting experience: my parents.

Although my daddy's presence was not consistent, his gifts were out of this world amazing! Christmas and my birthday were full of fun and excitement because I knew if I could not depend on him any other day, those two days were damn-near guaranteed to be a good time. If I asked him for random things here or there, he would fuss or give me a hard time at first, but he would usually cave into my desire for the newest and latest British Knights, my favorite school stationery sets, Caboodles, etc. I was a great student and handled my business, so it was hard to say no!

I loved calling my daddy and telling him good news, even if I had to deal with my heart dropping to the floor when *she* answered. It was just...*awkward*. I didn't know her, she really didn't take the time to get to know me, and I didn't trust anyone that was cool with breaking up families and homes.

I remember one time I was trying to call him to tell him I made the Principal's List, and my call was rejected multiple times. The phone never rang. It was an automated voice recording saying, "You cannot complete this call at this time." I ran to my mama's room and shared with her my disdain for not being able to contact him. She tried and got the same response.

We quickly got dressed and left the house. My mama pulled up to the nearest pay phone. I dropped a quarter into the slot, and quickly dialed my daddy's number and *she* answered, snickering on the phone. I asked to speak to my daddy. She passed him the phone, and I proceeded to tell him about my good news and asked why I had been blocked from calling him. He told me congratulations and that he was proud, but had no answer about why I was blocked from calling him. At that moment, I knew my daddy had *left*. A lot of things changed when *she* entered the picture and he was completely oblivious to it. Little did I know, I was changing too.

As I approached my teenage years, I realized he was the "money" man because that is what he presented. Therefore, I treated him as such. He made his presents available over his presence and because I was a very involved child growing up, I had a band fee, chorus fee, school fee, or some kind of fee due every other week. I began to notice that I would only call him when I needed something, not out of the sheer concern to see how he was doing. He taught me how to treat him because he valued presents over presence.

Of course, I wanted more from this daddy-daughter relationship, but he wasn't willing to give me more and to be honest, I eventually got tired of asking for it. As I reached my high school years, I realized I shouldn't have to beg my daddy for a relationship, so the relationship that I once knew with my daddy withered away to little or nothing. I saw him for who he truly was and no longer had expectations. This relationship set the tone as I grew up because my daddy taught me the importance of presence over presents. It was a life lesson I will never, ever, ever, forget.

<u>Takeaways</u>

1) Children love to receive gifts and will always be excited to get something they desire but presents will never outweigh presence. I can only remember a few of those gifts, but I remember all of the times he was present. Presence over presents ALWAYS.

2) Don't present yourself as the "money" parent. What you present is what your children will seek. We teach people how to treat us, even the little humans of the world.

Chapter 6

The Effects & Accountability

The effects of my daddy's decisions and dishonesty reared its ugly head one too many times. Something as simple as a wedding invitation that we never received nor were we privy to the fact a wedding was happening at all. We had to find out from a third party that he had married *her*, yet I was supposed to visit him and be happy as if "all is well." He unapologetically carried on as if nothing had happened, yet the effects were all around.

I even shared with him how I felt that he never advocated for us. What man thinks it is okay to only take one of his four children (yes, a second child was born while he was married to my mama) to the family reunions? What man thinks it is okay to take family pictures with his new wife and child without us AND put the pictures up around the house that we come to visit as if that is okay. Even if he had to take pictures with just us on one of those intermittent weekend visits...hell, be creative! Do you know what type of trauma that creates for a child? Sadly, he had no clue.

Dealing with him became vexatious and once I realized I could not do it alone, I sought therapy. As a college student, I still had questions and tried several times to have a conversation with my daddy, but my attempts were always met with aggression, defense, and anger. What I couldn't understand was why was he so damn mad. I had every right to be the "angry" one, yet I approached him in a very mature manner to discuss how his selfishness led to my hurt. His favorite line: "This is old stuff, why do we have to keep talking about old stuff?"

That statement alone let me know he was *still* clueless. I have a saying and it is "old stuff will remain current stuff if it is not dealt with appropriately along with willing participants, attached solutions, and genuine intentions." He clearly liked old stuff because he was not willing to make any adjustments, and once I accepted that he just couldn't be who I needed him to be, my life changed forever and the healing process began.

Seeking therapy was the best thing I could have ever done. There was a point in my life where I could not talk about my daddy without crying and being pissed off at him. I was disappointed and embarrassed about his choices, but once I started my sessions, I released the anger, the hurt, and everything in between. Anyone can hold a grudge, but it takes true character and courage to reach forgiveness. It was a necessary process over a two-year period of time that led to me forgiving him and being okay with the sincere apology I never received.

Takeaways

1) Defenseless communication can solve problems. Take YOU out of it. Insert accountability into the conversation, and mountains can be moved. Provide a safe space where children have the opportunity to voice their feelings the same way the mother or father gets the opportunity to do with their supportive family, friends, and/or therapist. Children need an outlet too, and fortunately, I had my granny and Mrs. Owens.

2) Vet the people you choose to be around your children. This is VERY important.

Does the person show genuine interest and concern for your children? Do they include your children in future plans? Is he/she capable of catering to your children's needs and not just YOURS? These are questions that need answers. Once vetted and if they are willing to accept your whole package—you and your children—proceed with introductions cautiously and with no pressure. An organic, natural progression is always better than a forced one.

3) Some men reduce the time they spend with their children from previous

relationships when they begin to be fruitful and multiply with another woman. It is as if the other "family" doesn't exist anymore. Children should never feel left out or as if they have been forgotten. It is not their fault how things turned out and it is up to the parents—their advocates—to include them in family gatherings, holidays, life celebrations, etc. This world is full of vultures and you should never want your children to be vulnerable to their ways.

4) Please keep in mind that children are not children forever. They become adults, begin to spread their wings,

and start to create their own families, so time is of the essence. It is a possibility that you may regret not spending time with them or have to face those tough, gut-wrenching questions one day. Get involved, include them in your life decisions, and create amazing, memorable experiences that will last for years to come.

Final Words

As heavy as this book was to write, it was indispensable that I share my story with you. It is my desire that it helps at least one family realize that divorce is an unspoken childhood trauma that shouldn't be taken lightly. As an educator, I have held one too many children in my arms sobbing profusely because no one felt the need to include them in the conversation about the dismantling that was occurring in their family.

They were in the midst of chaos; heartbroken and powerless, and their little lights were dimming. I slowed the pace of their breathing and the flow of their tears with some of the same soothing words my granny and teacher shared with me. Their innocent souls really only had one question, "why?" Yet no one took the time to answer because maybe, *just maybe*, they didn't know why either.

We have to learn how to accept our life experiences, good or bad. Our parents don't always get it right. They are human too and oftentimes have had traumatic experiences themselves that has had effects on their lives. My daddy clearly struggled as a father and as a husband, but the love has never wavered. Always remember, forgiveness is not something we do for other people, but instead what we do for ourselves.

#*TheBossyEducator* 🐦📷 @thebossyeducator

Inquiries: info@thebossyeducator.com

Website: TheBossyEducator.com